The Girl in the Midst of the Harvest

Also by KATHRYN STRIPLING BYER

Wildwood Flower
Black Shawl
Catching Light
Coming To Rest
Descent

The Girl in the Midst of the Harvest

Poems

KATHRYN STRIPLING BYER

Press 53
Winston-Salem

Press 53, LLC
PO Box 30314
Winston-Salem, NC 27130

First Edition

Cover design by Kevin Morgan Watson

Cover art, "Indian Corn Fantasy" Copyright © 2013
by Henrietta Ladson, used by permission of the artist.

Back cover art, "Du-Lu-S-Ti," by Sharyn Hyatt-Wade,
was the cover art for the original 1986 Texas Tech Press edition.
Used by permission of the artist.

Author photo by Corinna L. Byer

Printed on acid-free paper
ISBN 978-1-935708-92-6

For Jim and Cory,
& my mother and father

Acknowledgments

Permission from the following to reprint the poems listed is gratefully acknowledged.

The Arts Journal: "The Backwoods," "Search Party" (poems 2-8)
Carolina Quarterly: "Soap Opera"
The Georgia Review: "Morning" (formerly "Housewifery"), "Dusk" (formerly "Harvests")
The Greensboro Review: "My Beautiful Grandmother," "Afternoon"
The Hudson Review: "Cornwalking," "Elegy"
The Iowa Review: "Daughter," "Evening" (formerly "Afternoon")
Mossy Creek Journal: "Sunrise"
The Oconee Review: "I Inherit the Light of My Grandmother's House" (poems 1, 2, 4, 5), "Wings," "Peanuts"
Poetry: "Old Orchard Road Again," "Like a Mother Who Never Sleeps, Rain," "Wide Open, These Gates"
Southern Poetry Review: "Drought"
The Southern Review: "Siler's Bald"
This End Up Postcards: "Prayer"
Three Rivers Poetry Journal: Search Party" (opening poem)
The Uwharrie Review: "Ghost Story," "Glory"
The Virginia Quarterly Review: "The Carpenter"
Western Humanities Review: "Angels"
Windflower Almanac: "Kitchen Sink," "Potatoes"

"Cornwalking" and "Dusk" are dedicated to my brother.

For their unwavering belief in these poems, I want to thank my friends Isabel Zuber, Patricia Peters, Elizabeth Addison, Nancy Joyner, Hal Farwell, and Ed Krickel.

Epigraphs are from the following:

"That's Georgia," by Anita Pollitzer, *Saturday Review,*November 4, 1950.
Lisel Mueller, trans. *Selected Later Poems of Marie Luise Kaschnitz.* Copyright 1980 by Princeton University press. Excerpts from "Dear Sun" reprinted with permission of Princeton University Press.
Rainer Maria Rilke. *Poems from the Book of Hours.* Translated by Babette Deutsch. Copyright 1941 by New Directions Publishing Corp. Reprinted by permission of New Directions.

The Girl in the Midst of the Harvest, by Kathryn Stripling Byer, was originally published in cooperation with the Associated Writing Programs as an AWP Award Series Selection.

The Girl in the Midst of the Harvest

COMMENT BY JOHN FREDERICK NIMS
Judge for the 1985 Associated Writing Programs Award Series for Poetry

This is one of those rare books of poetry—earthy, sensuous, brave-spirited—that gives us the feeling of a full human life as vividly as a novel aspires to do. Here are scenes our eyes can focus on and all of our senses stir to—scenes that begin with girlhood on a Georgia farm, alive with its grumbling pigs and whispering corn tall enough to get lost in; scenes evoked by family memories that, like the words *great grandmother*, "carried the cadence of Genesis"; imagined scenes from lives of kinfolk who had pioneered in the Black Hills in the rough old days. As the years whirl by, there are scenes of the poet sitting down to oatmeal with her own young daughter, as beyond the window the sunlight transfigures an oak tree on Hawk Knob until it reminds her of Ghiberti's doors in Florence. By now the poet has gone far afield, as in a childhood poem she felt she might; she has ridden trains through the orange groves of Andalucia; she knows about political assassination in Central America. The final section, deeply emotional for all of its starkness, is a series in which she lives through the last days and death of a grandmother. In these poems we share in the lives of many human beings, the poet among them: a sturdy and enduring stock that can sing

> "All the good times are past and gone,
> Little darlin', don't weep no more…"

and yet sing it with courage and exhilaration.

BEFORE THE HARVEST—A PREFACE

In the work of Kathryn Stripling Byer we encounter a poetic voice which is unusually warm and intensely human. *The Girl in the Midst of the Harvest* presents a person who has mastered those roles society in the past marked out as woman's, as she moves on from *wife, mother, queen of the harvest* into a less explored terrain of identity and expression. The touching power and tenderness of these poems come in part from their courageous acceptance of what for most people is the inescapable. Many writers today partly avoid or only partially acknowledge those basics which the great masses of people "out there," before the T.V., beside the bassinet, accept but are unable to articulate. But Kathryn Byer is both a full human being, living to the limit every dimension of inheritance, every possibility of the past—and a full-scale poet, bringing this complete emotional world into verbal realization.

Kay Byer's thoughts are crowded with other presences: an Indian-like ancestress, lonely pioneer grandmothers, the rowdy driver of a truck over mountain ruts, the grandmother whose house burned, taking away certain key heirlooms but leaving in its invisible persistence a pattern of womanly identity within which to reconstruct life. This poet's imagination is unable (and unwilling) to escape its function as link between the world that was and that which is coming to be. Unlike current society, which seems to live with a growing fault-line between the past and itself, so that one day soon the continent containing our history will break off from the California of the present and sink into the sea, Kay Byer inhabits an unfractured world. She has her wounds, of course. She is loving and therefore vulnerable, and even for this daughter of the harvest, the models of the past are, though necessary, inadequate. Yet like persons who have not lost contact with their own home landscape and earlier life, she has a sense of some original scope and emotional possibility. We feel that psychic elbow-room which is so refreshingly present in nineteenth century writers such as Walt Whitman and Mark Twain. This poet has the completeness and courage to move on from those more intuitive life-activities associated with ancestors, husband, child and garden, into questions of selfhood and significance most of us are too distracted (or too crippled) to pursue.

I suggest that Kay Byer, perhaps because she *is* so richly endowed with memory, family, and natural environment, has the hardihood to face real loneliness. Her imaginative re-creation of the western travels of a great grandmother (sufficiently mythologized to serve as a generic model of one facing female identity as a pioneer) provides us with poetry of a daring, a directness, and yet of a mystery appropriate to a voyage into the final issues.

> You could be anyone's daughter. Who
> are you? You stumble into the mesquite
> still looking for one perfect skull
> with a family resemblance which you will hold
> up to the light. Through the holes
> that were once her eyes you see the sky come
> to meet you, panoramic as history.

Beyond the debate over male/female roles and past/present/future, she makes us feel what it is to be elementally conscious in the American vastness.

Thus, Kay Byer gives us starkness, desert, dry bone, and she gives us fullness, fruitfulness, gives us a terrible western silence versus the corn talking as only its green tongues can. We see the girl in high spirits then and the grown woman knitting, making more links in the chain which is bondage as well as empowerment. She gives us then and now, before and after: husband and child and garden in a sweet, strained present behind which we see the roping genetic strands, both biological and psychological. Like the magnet at the center of great arcing lines of force, she makes of her position in a house on a ridge of the Appalachian mountains a vantage point overlooking our current situation. The most compelling issues of the day intersect somewhere outside Sylva, N.C., in the head of a young woman named Kay Byer, and become imaginative vision and song.

Technically, these poems live up marvelously to the fullness of life of the subject matter and to the rigorous intelligence of this quest for selfhood. These poems are formal, fecund, and self-critical. Their rhythms can thrust out singingly, can careen with the mountain truck over ruts and hummocks. And their movement can pierce and separate, can slice like steel. We see ghosts, angels, storms, drought, fire, a bitter death in Central America, and we hear them too. Like her vision, Kay Byer's song is a rare combination of richness and elegance, the full laugh and riot of good times and the whisper of the Beyond. In all respects, we feel here the balance of the poet fully empowered for her task and shrinking from and omitting nothing. What should be sung is warbled, that to be praised is hymned, that to be mourned is movingly elegized, and that to be execrated is hissed, made vivid as a wickedness we too sadly recognize. But this poet counsels us neither to Utopian dream, escapist fantasy, retreat into selfishness, nor despair. Her poems say strength, say realism, say endurance, say love, say richness, against the threatening desolation. Rereading this book, I feel that the greatest aid we might wish toward a more hopeful future would be a wider dissemination of this poet's capacity for valuing deeply and permanently those things which *should* most profoundly matter.

I would not wish, by singling out a few poems, to suggest that the reader should pay less than devoted and repeated attention to all in this book. Yet I also wish to record my admiration and love of poems such as "Wide Open, These Gates," "Cornwalking," "New Year's Eve," and of "Ashes," "Thieves," "Cloud," "Sunrise"—indeed, of the whole last section, a sequence describing the burning of her grandmother's house and the self-reconstruction growing out of that conflagration. These strong, lovely lyrics I have named and those which surround and extend them carry to us the voice of an important new poet.

James Applewhite
Durham, North Carolina
February, 1986

I
The Girl in the Midst of the Harvest

Already ripening barberries grow red,
the ageing asters scarce breathe in their bed.
Who is not rich, with summer nearly done,
will never find a self that is his own.

R. M. Rilke, from *Das Stundenbuch*

Wide Open, These Gates

Going down the road feeling good, I snap
my fingers. Hear, hear! At an auction my father
bid sixty-five dollars for a fat Hampshire pig
just by rubbing his nose. When my grandfather
scattered his seed to the four corners, corn stood up
tall as his hat brim. My grandmother's sheets
flapped like bells on the line. Crabbed youth,
crab apple, crepe myrtle, I mumble

as I shuffle downhill, my crabbed youth
behind me like gnats singing. I've come a long way
from what's been described as a mean and starved
corner of backwoods America. That has a ring
to it. Rhythm, like my grandmother's hands
in the bread dough. Her food made the boards creak,
my grandfather mellow. He had a wild temper
when he was a young man. Most folks talk too much,
he'd say, aiming slow spit at a dung beetle.
He never mumbled. Sometimes he talked nonsense

to roosters and fierce setting hens. My nonsense coos
like a dove. Goodbye swallowtails cruising
the pigpen. Goodbye apple dumplings. Goodbye
little turkeys my grandmother fed with her fingers.
Big Belle was a nanny goat. Holler "Halloo"
after sundown and all the cows come home. Some words
are gates swinging wide open, and I walk on through
one more summer that like this road's going
down easy. The gnats sing, and I'm going
to sing. One of these days I'll be gone.

Cornwalking

This summer because of so little cleared ground
we have only two rows at the edge
of the garden. And yet even now
when I kneel to pick beans
I can hear the corn whisper, "Hither come,
hither come," so I put down my basket

and walk the short rows
pretending it's Georgia midsummer
and the corn at my grandfather's farm's
fit to lose myself in

as I did a few times, losing sight
of all fences
and cousins
and stalking straight out of this world
down the streets of the corn kingdom,
sassy and satisfied,
twining its green worms around my heart's finger
for luck in love, kicking up dirt
for the smell of it. Cornblossom Maiden

I was, with the corn itch
and squirt of the kernel in both eyes
from testing a ripe ear. So what did I care
if a thundercloud crept from the forest
and waited for me to come out
again? Neither my cousins
nor my grandmother ringing the bell in the backyard
for me to come home on the double

could find me once
I reached the middle of three thousand corn rows
to sing at the top of my lungs
with the gathering wind in the corn itself
singing, "We are growing everywhere.
What is the world but our song?"

Daughter

The whole world lay before me those Saturdays.
In good weather I could sit down beneath any tree
and for half a day gather a tow sack too full of pecans
to be carried. Then there was no reason
to hurry. My mother, a few yards away,
let me dream. At the next tree

old Autry sat slumped on an oil can
still mooning for Lester who'd left home for good
this time. Worked both her hands to the bone
for him she had, she said and considered her fingers
as if she still wanted to grab a strong oak limb
and stir one last washpot about to boil over.
No wonder sad Sugar Boots sang the blues
all afternoon, five months gone
and no good man to find. Not one good man
in three hundred miles. No one spoke

while she sang. There was nothing to do
but to listen. The telephone wires festooned over the fields
hummed with messages. Soon all
the pigs in the county were rattling their feed troughs
for supper and all together too
slowly the trees in the distance were turning
to clouds. All that time I was waiting to turn

seventeen. Hand in
and hand out again. Hand
halfway between the full sack
and the ground. I remember

the message I almost forgot
I knew. I have my grandfather's word
on an acre of black dirt, my father's
on four hundred more. What
they lost is not lost. Here I am.
When I look up, the future's a field for me.
I am the girl in the midst of the harvest.

I am the harvest.

Dusk

My father made the birds fly overhead
that afternoon in late fall when he lifted me
above the weeds as tall as I was then
into a wagon load of hay. There at the field's edge
while he whistled, restless in the cold,
I watched the shadows of the nearby pines
trail the woods like tattered clouds.

He brooded on the silent stalks
and never noticed me while all his wagons
turned toward home at dusk. Why do I still believe
I saw him standing by the sea of stubble
waving me goodbye until I reached the gatepost
where I sent his goodbye back across the weeds?

He disappeared into his ruined rows
with the dust that sifted through the dying light.
He left me reaping shadows for his hand until the branches
at the road's bend hid the field. That's when
the swallows rising from a roadside thicket
streaked the early darkness with their wings
before they turned and followed sunset out of sight.

I saw their feathers gleam like grain thrown on the wind.

The Backwoods

Great-grandmother carried the cadence of Genesis.
Girl cousins up late at family reunions,
we made her an Indian, although her forebears
were Irish. Before her lay darkness, the empty fields
barren as desert until she came forward,
the sweat on her high cheekbones gleaming like eyes
we imagined surrounding her, bob-cat and red fox,
the last of the sleek, singing wolves. Every evening
she shouldered her hoe and walked home
through the tasselling corn. The Good Lord only knows
what bare feet stalked the backwoods in those days,
what waited behind every woodpile! She brought forth
a daughter with black hair that never curled.
Shy as a fieldmouse, that girl fell in love
with a man scything hay in the twilight. They kissed
twice. A moment she stood in her white dress
and smiled back at us, then she grew fat and sighed
in the kitchen. Four daughters she bore,
and the three who survived scarlet fever
wove grass in their brown hair and danced every night
with the fireflies. They galloped on wild horses
bareback until they got married and gave birth
to us, Southern Belles who could sit in a parlor
all evening and never complain. We could faint
in a handsome man's arms. We could charm
a stone wall. But we never forgot the back door,
how to disappear into the darkness, our crinolines rustling
like cornstalks between our legs. We told
this story so well, we inherit its black earth
where women hoe all night, inscrutable as Indians.

Peanuts

1

"Crack your knuckles in church
with the boys and your knucklebones
turn unrespectable, same as if you were to dig
in the dirt with Lobelia
and hide your black hands out of pure
Sunday shame. Dirty fingernails
give you a bad name, and dirty
feet shuffle down back
alley streets. Better cover your legs
with a sheet while you're picking
off those gritty peanuts and shake
yourself good, girl,

before you come
inside. I don't want any sand
on my sofa, or swimming like fleas
in my sink, idle hands
make an old woman weep, so you rinse
every peanut six times, dump
them into this hard-boiling
water. Now add a big
handful of salt. I tell you what
is the truth, the secret
of good tasting peanuts is salt."

They walked me up
and down that dusty road
eating her peanuts
until we were thirsty as dogs.
At a puddle
Sylvester on all fours
drank like a dog
while we laughed. I took
my thirsty tongue home
and drank her iced tea
from a tall crystal glass
though I slurped
and my sweaty blouse stank
to high heaven.

Angels

We sang Adeste Fideles while
clouds darkened over my grandfather's
farmhouse. What angels
we were, my three cousins caressing
their bride dolls, and I, the soprano
in front keeping time because
I sang the loudest. The nerve
of somebody (my deaf aunt?)
to whisper, "Tornado"! We wouldn't stop
singing till hailstones came
clattering down on the tin roof the way
in the movies Comanches charge out of a hill
like an avalanche. "Open a window,"
my grandfather yelled while we ran
for the root cellar, clutching our candles
like converts. The house howled
with wind as the Angel of Death thundered
on to the next town where (so
it's been told every year since that
Christmas night) two men were raised
by the whirlwind and set down
a mile away, babbling of light
at the end of a tunnel,
the buzzing of ten thousand angels.

Elegy

Again it's the night of the shivering stars
and ice sprouting under the hooves
of the cattle my mother says
she counted while she was driving
to town where he lay turning cold
as the stiff grasses. (How many
cows, I asked years later. Twenty-one,
she answered. Twenty-one cows huddled
under the sad moon.) He died on my birthday
at three in the morning, attempting to go
to the bathroom one last time
alone, the official Deathstory,
but I don't for one word of this goodbye
lyric believe he was not
bound, like any brave grandfather,
out the back door where a man ought
to take his last piss, aiming
straight at the bull's-eye of darkness.
He lifted himself to his full height
and strode two miraculous steps. Maybe
three, like a poor country boy walking home
on a night such as this, singing "Darlin'
don't weep no more." How her tears must have shone
in the moonlight until she reached up with the hem
of her apron! Tonight I'm that girl
left behind who has sworn she will not weep
one pretty tear more, though the autumn leaves
fall from the trees like his hands
to the cold bathroom floor and tomorrow
I wake up another year older.
Again I have drunk too much brandy to mourn
for the bare feet on which he set forth
as if told he must take up his mattress
and walk away, praising each step of the journey.

Old Orchard Road Again

This winter there's not much to do.
He can drive till the gas runs out, walk home
on mud frozen into a sculpture of tiretracks
and hoofprints, the thud of his boots flushing
quail from the underbrush. Nobody's waiting
to scold him when he peels his socks
from a ripe blister. Birds in the rafters
stir all night like warnings he's almost forgotten.
*Lie still while the doctor is talking. That window
stays shut. Don't walk out in the blinding sun.*

No need to worry now, he'd rather drive
long as he can hear Hank Williams singing his faded love
over the rattle of rusty chrome. Pigs fat on nothing
but corn cobs and solitude lie straight ahead
like temptation he can't resist. One lonesome honk
of the horn and they stand up like drunks,
strewing shoats from their flabby teats. Bouncing clear
off the seat spilling its stuffing around him,
he yells out the window, "Here's mud in your eye!"
but the sows stagger off into dust his truck's churned
up so thick he can't find his way back
to the gate. Surely Hank never sang such a sad song
as wheels spinning into the sand. Damn the static!
Where's Orange Blossom Special? He strips his gears
clean as the sugar cane stalks he sucked dry
every summer and charges through blackberry thorns
onto Old Orchard road again. Praise be the cattle gap
clattering under him! Perched on a water trough
three girls are waving their straw hats beribboned with ivy
and broom sedge. He no longer cares why
they're waiting here, clad in their pale cotton dresses
as if it's dead summer and somehow the sun
never disappeared into their childhood.
What took you so long, they call,
climbing in back with the oil cans and greasy tools.

Look out for low limbs, he motions to them through
the rear window, grinning when he sees a dirty foot dart
under petticoats. Why should he mind
if they're not wearing stockings and black
lace-up shoes? Let them wiggle their toes
all the way to the house almost hidden
in trumpet vines. Through the broken glass
he sees a white curtain yearning toward apple trees
and as his head bows against branches closing
around them, he thinks of the birch rod
held over them all in the school room,
his sentence prayers muttered at morning devotion.
Thank you for green grass.
Thank you for clear water.
Thank you for eyes that cannot look too long at the sun.

The Carpenter

From ashes I rebuild my grandfather's house.
It is slow labor. Whatever is left
I must gather. My hip pockets bulge
with coals the roof scattered like seed.
I hoist tangled wire onto my shoulders
and stumble forth, huffing and puffing,
to search the debris for a nail straight enough
to be hammered. As soon as I find it,
I pound with conviction but no skill.
I hold up my battered blue thumb to the sky
and I curse as magnificently
as my grandfather ever did, calling on
bird, beast, and cosmos to judge his incompetence.
Tears streak my dirty cheeks. Each day I quit
and each day I start over again,
using buckets of glue if I must, and
a patience I hardly knew I had inherited.

I have one window already aloft
in my grandmother's kitchen. Above the remains
of her teacups and crockery, it frames the oak
sifting light through its branches
like wheat. If the glass is cracked
I do not notice. By spring
I will see the big kettle secure
on the stove and the stove-pipe ascending.
The bread will rise endlessly. Butter will come
in the earthenware churn. Let the roof wait
for winter. My grandfather's house always
was airy with a sly breeze,
the pig stink all night long in summer.
I slept under cracks where the winking rain
entered, so why should I mind
the bad weather? I work best when I take

my time, coaxing woolly worms into a tin can
and letting them go again, dreaming
the night sky unfolds like a blueprint I learn
to read. Sometimes I dawdle with scrap iron
and bed-springs until it is dawn. Unembarrassed,
I sing the old ditties. Hey diddle-
diddle, I dance by the light of the moon
and feel lonely, already at home
here. I talk to the rubble. I swear
by the toil of my two clumsy hands I will

make of this junk-pile a dwelling place
yet. When I hammer the last nail straight
into the last sagging beam, I will
spit on the edge of my shirt and sit down
on a barrel to scrub my face clean.
I will not look my Sunday-best,
but I cannot wait forever.
The hinges will creak as I open the front door
and call out my grandfather's name.
In the silence that answers, I step
slowly over the threshold,
believing that each board supports me.

My Beautiful Grandmother

died ugly,
wasted with hunger,
her arms black and blue from the needles,
the last ones she took up
when she stopped embroidering pink cornucopias
on square after square of white cotton.
Nobody could coax her to eat after six years
of morphine. Not even my father.

She'd wanted to leave
for a long time, she wanted
the mountains, the cool
air, the sky coming down
like a good sleep, she wanted

to go back to where she had been
when she wore the red plume in her hat
and sat pointing the toe of her shoe
at the camera. Oh

she was a dashing one
all the men said and say
still if you ask them. Her mind was as quick
as the stitch of a sparrow's wing.
Coming and going,
she made sure her petticoats rustled.
A flirt and a good one she was
and so square-jawed and German she looked
like the belle of some old-country tavern.
Her laugh was a yodel.

She wasn't the belle of that small town
in Georgia. But, stubborn,
she tried what she knew worked
a little while. She fell in love
with a young man whose letters she saved
in a hatbox. I opened one
once. It read: "Darling,
my heart counts the moments
until we are wed!" Then
it crumbled like stale bread.
The rats had gnawed whole words away.
Such a bride,
such a bride, all the townspeople said
and forgot her. I grew up remembering

I was her granddaughter. And it's been years
I've spent leaving that small town in Georgia
where my beautiful grandmother stayed.

Ghost Story

She stalks these mountains
in high button shoes
and the silk skirt she wore
when she flirted with cowboys
and wild Irish miners
who came north to strike
it rich quick in the Black Hills
where winter was fiercer
than even the coldest ones here
in the tame Appalachians
she later called home.
On her deathbed she sighed
for the mountains of Brasstown,
Dahlonega, even the ridge
of the Balsams she'd seen
only once from a passing
car. Thirty years
she cursed the heat
of south Georgia, the flies,
and the infernal gossip
that branded her. Unsmiling
she walked the small streets.
Now she stalks these mountains
from Big Fork to Snowbird,
her shoe buttons gleaming,
her silk skirt a cloud
trailing after the full moon.

Drought

Dirt, always
the smell of dry dirt
while I sweated through summer,
my father complaining about blue sky
stretching all the way west into Arkansas.
Dry ice they tumbled
from planes sometimes. Thunder
and strong wind might come

but no rain. Pigs grumbled
from sun-up to sundown. The cows stood
immobilized under the oak trees,
their turds turning black as the biscuits I burned
while I daydreamed. Wherever I played I saw corn dying
year after year, teased by dust devils
leaving their tidings between my toes
and in ring after ring round my neck. I scrubbed
ring after ring of black dirt from the bathtub
at night. I got used to my own sweat

and so much hot weather
the fragile petunias collapsed
by mid-afternoon. Hold up
your shoulders straight, I heard a thousand times.
Books on my head, I'd be sent out
to water the flowers as if that would help salvage
anything but my good humor, the smell of wet dirt

my reward, for which I knew I ought
to be grateful, as now nearly twenty years later I am
grateful, thirsty as dry land

I stand upon, stoop-shouldered,
wanting a flash flood to wash away Georgia
while I aim the water hose into a sad patch of pansies.
Nothing has changed. I can still hear my father complain
while my mother cooks supper and I swear to leave
home tomorrow. In some places dams burst
but I don't believe it. Here water is
only illusion, an old trick
light plays on the highway that runs north
through field after field after field.

II
SEARCH PARTY

*"That was my country—terrible
winds & a wonderful emptiness."*

Georgia O'Keefe

You ask me to write of my mother's life, notes for your family records in
Ireland. Cousin, I find that a difficult task. Of my father you doubtless have heard
many stories, for he was a daring, perhaps even foolhardy, man. But my mother was
more like the gold he spent most of his life seeking. Hidden. She came with her
parents from Stettin, spoke nothing but German at first. Legend has it that she
was the first white child into the Black Hills. How she loved that story! And others
she told us—of gunfights and lynchings, of hard-drinking miners who courted her,
promising gold rings and red satin shoes. As she aged she grew silent, as if she'd
gone back to the wilderness, lost to her husband and children. The times I have
tried to imagine her thoughts! And I know, even as I am writing this letter, that she
is a stranger for whom I will always be searching, with sand in my eyes and the sun
beating down on the trail she has taken....

—from a letter my grandmother might have written, circa 1920

In three days the buzzards come.
They clean up the mess
of death. Sun does
the rest and so quickly

the skull fills with sand
like a porcelain bowl. In a month every bone shimmers
under the moon, a spectacular heap
in the desert somewhere between home
and the Black Hills. She never came back.

An old man found the wagon. The letters
are lost, and her diary ends
at the border of Tennessee. You have the Bible

she left to you, lines scrawled
like prophecy over the frontispiece, "Dust is
the hand that has written these words. I will wait
for you, Dearest, in Deadwood." You set out

to find her. You carry your dust
to her dust. On this journey no maps
chart the landscape. The sun blinds,
the wind mocks you. If you want to live,

you eat lizards, suck water from cactus
and when you lean over a clear pool
at last, you are unrecognizable.
You could be anyone's daughter. Who
are you? You stumble into the mesquite
still looking for one perfect skull
with a family resemblance which you will hold

up to the light. Through the holes
that were once her eyes you see the sky come
to meet you, panoramic as history.

1

I am a woman of few words.
The black snake needs no conversation.
The sun needs no coaxing to come forth.
The rocks are indifferent to curses.
Have words ever made my life easier,
the thread I knot stronger?

My mother was German. I left her.
My daughter considers me dead.
To my grandchildren
I could tell stories of arrow-heads
lodged in a man's heart.
But what I know best is the emptiness.
In it the wind sings of nothing

but rocks crumbling,
roots letting go.

2

I escaped with a hairbrush,
a needle, the locket in which Mamma
scowled her admonishment, "Do not

what the Lord frowns upon."
I walked into the darkness and fell.
When I woke I heard water,

as if my own blood flowed beyond me.
How long I lay hearing water wear down the black
canyon I cannot remember. Then hooves

on the stone and a man
stood above me in gray fur. He raised
my head. I saw his eyes: empty
space. He said nothing
but lifted me onto his horse.
In his cabin he bathed me. By lamplight
my wedding ring shone. He asked no questions,
and I could not speak.
I could cook. I could lie in a bed.
I kept my silence
and listened at nightfall for water.

3

Deadwood,
the very name wearied me
but I kept going.
A woman must follow,
must follow,
my footsteps repeated
through Tennessee
Arkansas, the wagon wheels

creaked like my mother's
voice, be
a good mother,
be a good wife,

be a strong woman. Now Mamma,
you would not know me,
my face baked brown as a clay pot.
I have grown stronger

than you can imagine.
So strong I say to you, "Leave me
alone," and you vanish
like smoke up the flue. I am

always alone. And I walk where I want
in this strange land, attempting
to stare with no memory
when the black hawk descends
to the neck of the hare.

4

My daughter, this letter
will never arrive.
You will search for me someday
but you will not find me.

For now, cut long chains of identical dolls.
At the keyboard play Humoresque fiercely.
Do not let the metronome goad you.
The way out is always through narrow doors
sky opens up in the trees.
Know those doors never shut.

Know I dare not remember
the hem of your cradle dress,
your small fingers clutching my nightgown,
your mouth,

and your toes I unwrapped every morning
as if they were gold coins I hoarded.

5

While green ebbed and flowed
in the forest, I sat in my room
thinking barrenness better
than washing away. But the rice
at my wedding fell.
And rain, so much rain

the old women laughed, raising
their glasses to prophesy sons,
many sons. I was not sick,

yet during confinement
my mother tied garlic around my neck
and invoked every ghost
of poor women who'd died giving birth
as a warning. No wonder
the child almost choked on the cord,
I almost lost all
my blood. When I turned

from the cradle one day
out of weariness, watching clouds pass
like boats on the river,
she chided me, "You want your own way."

How could I deny it?
"You are too stubborn,"
she said. "You will be left alone
in your old age."

Yes, Mamma. I sit at the table
and stare at the empty bowl.
There is no supper.

6

Winter rose.

Like a foreign word
this stitch repeats itself
loop after loop and I find
I have made three good circles,
a center,
two leaves,

and my fingers have not lost
their language. I first saw this pattern
on coverlets under my chin. It appeared

on the kerchief my mother held,
waving goodbye. To the hem
of my grandmother's wedding dress
white roses clung like the snow
that fell endlessly, for in Stettin
no roses bloomed in the snow.
Ever after she sat by the fire
stitching roses on every rough edge.

Should I visit her, she would look up
only once to say, "Liebchen,
come here. I will show you a good
morning's work." In the snow

of Stettin, little Grandmother sat,
stitching roses red
as her own restless blood.

You think you have found her?
You have not found her.
Do you think this dust is her body,
these bones wrapped in tumbleweed

hers? You will find her in water
you draw from the well,
in the dusty streets no one is travelling,
in the women who welcome you
onto their porches, say nothing,
then turn away
when you look down at their hands.

In the silence
you find her

and you lose her
again and again.

If you follow the road
she has taken,
you come to a hut where smoke
curls from the chimney.
You open the door.
There is bread on the table,
a jar of cool water, a clean plate,
your name scrawled in ash
on a napkin. Starved woman,
you sit down and eat.
There is no one at home here but you.

III
HOMECOMING

We believe the time has come
To stop loving anyone
And give up our planet
Let it drift
Cold among cold satellites.

But the undiminished
Daily witness
Of lips kissing
Dear sun
Good earth
Forever and ever
Knows better.

Marie Luise Kaschnitz, from "Dear Sun."
Translated by Lisel Mueller

Daily Witness

1

MORNING

The pine bough framed as usual
by my kitchen window sags with snow.
As I drink coffee in this house that hugs the hill
against the wind, what we have brought
together under one roof rights itself around me.

If I tried to fool myself,
I'd say a place for everything
and everything in place—the soup cans in my pantry,
Rembrandt's windmill framed above your easy chair,
my own face framed by pots of philodendron
while I look for spider webs that spring like weeds

across the walls. But even as I scrape the dishes
clean of one more breakfast's scraps,
the clouds beyond me crumble into afternoon.
Just yesterday I watched the last leaves claw back
at the cold before they snapped their stems
like all the rest. They say it's woman's work

to keep back what she knows, the boredom
of these mornings that are swept on soon enough.
They say it has its own rewards.
But listen. Such a stillness
in the corners of my house!
Sometimes I want to lie down in it,
sleep as we did last night while the snow fell
on our roof, deliberately as dust.

2

AFTERNOON

I pull yarn looped
around my needle
through a stitch and move
on to another. Single
crochet's what they call
it and for larger stitches
there are more loops
you must gather and
control. You've double,
treble, double treble
crochet as the stitches
hook into a sweater
or a shawl or what's more
common, rippled afghans
if you're patient.
Making something out of
almost nothing, some
new pattern from
a ball of yarn takes
hours. Days. Takes dawn
till dark. My mother
did it, and her
mother and her mother's
mother fashioned doilies
out of thin white thread
while I looked on. She
said such fingerwork
calmed women's nerves by
making them take pains
to pass the time. It's true

the chains link up
so quickly you may hardly
notice when it's time
to turn. All afternoon
I pull yarn looped
around my needle through
these countless stitches
cradled in my arms.

EVENING

If these leaves between

the light and where we lie
together almost sleeping, burning
themselves out the same,

the same as always
though I stroke your thigh
that lies against my own

until its dark hair warms
my palm like pinestraw kindling, if
this should be too much

on my mind, the fading
not the fire, for me to dare
ask what will happen

to us, please forgive me.
But don't look at me like that,
as if your eyes can't help

but hold an hourglass of light
in each, and light already six o'clock
and sinking. Makes me tired

enough to turn away from you
sometimes, from love
itself that makes me want

the two of us alive forever.

Soap Opera

My neighbor has slender hips,
hair shining straight
down (mine curls),
and a blue-eyed lover
with a deep voice that I overhear
on purpose saying, "Pam,
come here," or saying,
"Look." But when I look,
between the branches of the pine trees
I see nothing. She laughs
in the shadows like a ghost
who sounds familiar.

Once I laughed too loud
because I had a brown-eyed lover
with a deep voice saying
softly many things that I could tell
you if I chose. My
next door neighbor's wife
was jealous (locked him out
one night for staring
in my window), and the Baptists
in the blue house
on the corner prayed for me.
Those were the days

I wore my dresses short
and drove too fast
around the curve my neighbor takes
at eighty every noon,
her hair blown like a battleflag.
But I go slowly now,
am in no hurry, having come
to where there's no place else

to go. Got married,
that is, to the man
I drove too fast to get to.
Got my happy ending.

May my neighbor get hers.

Wings

My daughter does not sleep as the books say
she will, from feeding
to feeding, at four hour intervals.
Placed in her cradle, she screams
at me, teary woman I see in the mirror
who's wringing her hands as I do
in bad dreams: a bird is trapped
inside the house, I cannot find my way
out of here. Let me go to the windows
this morning as if it were spring and sit down
by their bright, wordless spaces.

They comfort me. Wiser than books
they profess nothing, merely allow me to see
in the branches two field sparrows
making their small celebration with such noisy energy
I feel ashamed to sing lullabyes,
praying for sleep. When the gray light

comes too early into our bedroom, invading
the cobwebby corners where dust I have not touched
for weeks will be waiting for many
weeks more, marking time
like my daughter whose wails greet each new day
with gusto, I stumble from bed
asking, "What am I doing here?"
Women build nests,
don't they? Who was it told me that?
How long ago? He was heading west,
wasn't he? Looking for freedom,
he said, and a girl in a sleeping bag,
sexy and childless. I yawn
and sit down with my daughter. A year ago
I rode a train through the orange groves of Andalucia,

not seeing a thing for the darkness. At dawn
a white village passed out of my life like the heron
I saw taking flight from the pasture before
I stopped looking and climbed with my heavy books
onto the school bus. I try to imagine those narrow streets
under the sun, how the women walk through them at noon,
singing simply of wind lifting long, dusty skirts,
but I see nothing—only the sky looking so empty

it could hold everything.
I want to hurl myself into it.
It is the sky over Spain
and New Mexico. It is the sky over cow pastures.
It is the same sky I see in my daughter's eyes
turning toward light and what light
always promises: wings and more wings.

Like a Mother Who Never Sleeps, Rain

wants to fill up the ditches
and chicken coops till there is nobody left

in the world but herself mumbling, "Buckles
and laces for sale. Pretty buckles

and laces." How can I pretend
I don't hear when this yearning for keys

in my breastpocket, books cradled
under my scarf makes me stand for too long

at the window where I can find nothing
to give to my daughter but words for what's wet

and unwelcoming? Old Mother Hubbard,
I've whistled home stray dogs

and danced with a billy goat,
gone round the mulberry bush till I'm dizzy

and yet she will think of me sad by a shut window
wanting to drive away into the sky

I can't see in the gray water flooding
the streets. She wants Snow White awakened,

a kiss on both cheeks. I want wind
on my face. We are caught

in a story with no happy ending. Rain
always comes back singing

pretty lies. Where is the sky,
the way out of this house where I hold her

so tightly she cries out against
me, brushing my lips with her eyelashes?

Frost

"Shake the cold from our hands," you call, running ahead
of me onto the frozen grass. Look, in the garden
your father wrests vines from a tripod of bamboo stakes.
Okra's grown weary with mourning another year
gone and just yesterday, Darling,
they wore yellow buds in their hair. Like you

twisting a puny chrysanthemum into your tangles
and galloping off on a broomstick. Down Caney Fork
scarecrows come hobbling like old soldiers
leaving their cornfields. They'll sit by the river
and talk about what the crows told them: a hard winter
coming. Those windy crows, all they keep saying
is *cold, cold,* and when I see clouds swept
like ice down the creek, I believe them
too easily. Why must the maple leaves rattle

Remember me, as if someday
I'll forget there were thousands came
falling the morning I felt for the first time you
shiver inside me, no fish as I thought you would be
but a mouse in its burrow? Now you sit in sand
and make birthday cakes, blowing out candles
that aren't there. I blow on my hands
like an old woman taking no heed of a child
who believes time can be shaken from her like water.

Heaven

If for a moment the oak tree transfigured
by sun crowning Hawk Knob reminds me of Florence
again and Ghiberti's bronze doors into Paradise,
why do I slurp my black coffee unceremoniously?

I crave the hand raised in blessing,
the open hand waiting. But what of my own hands
that set out this food for my daughter?
She shoves them away like the breakfast she won't eat.
Her hand in the honey bowl mocks me.
Just one little kiss?
She sucks each sticky finger and grins
while the last of the summer flies drone

in the kitchen. (I think
of my deathbed, the flies on the ceiling
I'll count while I wait for her,
blonde woman dawdling in roadside cafes
where the jukebox plays love,
helpless love.) Little acorn

that grew in me, out of me,
how she would laugh if I told her my hands
stroked her body as though it were bronze
growing warm in the Florentine sun:
Mary's face turned away from the angel,
the trees over Christ as he beckons to Lazarus.
"Window," she cries, reaching out

to its light.
"Closed," I say,
"Winter's coming. The pretty leaves
fall. Hurry, eat all you can before
I take your oatmeal away."
She refuses to listen.
Her oatmeal turns hard as I told her it would.
Cold and hard, though
a heaven of Tuscan leaves trembles beyond us.

Solstice

for PCP

Riding home on the subway,
you tried not to look at the old woman
mumbling in Spanish, "Mi corazón,
mi corazón de soledad."

Longest dark. Hours after sunset
and no coffee left in the pot, you are saying
your rosary, each word a wing beat against
blackened window glass. (Mother of Letting Go,

Mother of Dust, Holy Mother of Mother's
Hearts) Outside, the lights of New York
gleam like candles, burning till dawn
for the souls of the lost.

"It is easy to pray to her,
she is so human," you told me last night,
though your voice on the long-distance line
stammered, trying to clarify something

you feared I'd dismiss as no more
than nostalgia, old charm
against darkness. I stared at the crèche
where a virgin in wooden robes knelt

while you spoke of her blood seeping
into the straw, how her hand,
holding close to the child's face
a guttering candle-stub, trembled.

Then silence. I thought the line
dead till I heard a match strike
for your cigarette. "Who knows,"
you sighed, watching smoke find

its way to the ceiling.
"Perhaps there is such a thing as grace,
the smallest twig kindling,
the empty hearth filling with light."

Santiago the Fisherman

In the month of His birth,
the Great Fisherman you
worshipped, huddled at mass
with your wife and nine children,
you were too trusting. They
came with their cameras
and deadlines. You rowed them
across to the bodies
stacked under wild grapevines.
They scribbled their notes
and their shutters clicked.
Truth, they explained, now
the truth will be told,
how this government murders
its people. You nodded,

so glad to be helpful.
The woman reached out for
your hand and said, "God bless
you, Good Santiago."
"Feliz Navidad,"
they called, driving away
to their telephones. That night
your wife shook with fear. "They
will kill you," she whimpered.
Your daughters' hands trembled
when they lit the morning
fire. They spilled your coffee.
They burned bread. You threw down
the food you could not eat
and left for the river.
No women there. Women,
how they made a man lose his way
in deep water! You drifted along
with the current and waited.

The truck rumbled into
your village next evening.
The captain said, "Someone
has told me a secret,
a rare fish I wish you to help
me catch. I hear you know
many things, Wise Santiago.
I make you a good offer.
Come with me" You shrugged.
You climbed in the truck
and looked down at your family.
Even your daughters were brave
for once. Even your wife,
who stared over your
head at the rising moon.

They found your body at
midnight, your throat slit.
Your sons knelt beside you
and cradled your bloody
head. Somebody loosened
your bound ankles. Bearing
you home, they heard voices
alongside the river
and many boats rowing
to some destination
they feared. Soon the newsmen
returned. "What has happened,"
they asked, "to our friend
Santiago?" Your wife
wept. Your sons stammered

into the microphone,
"Soldados, soldados."
Everyone nodded. "Si,
soldiers are everywhere.
How could he hope to
escape them, the old fool?"
And so in the month of
Our Lord's birth your death is
a sad story broadcast
at dinnertime, after
the stock market rallies
and special reports on
what's selling in toy stores
where mothers do battle
for bodies of stuffed dolls
adopted like children.

December, 1983

New Year's Eve

We kneel at the hearth, blowing hard
to make wet wood kindle. Rain ends this old year
of drought in my father's fields littered with cornstalks
like corpses he would not plow under.
"The last days," he likes to say,
quoting Isaiah. "Behold, they shall be as stubble."

Why were we spared? On our mountainside
blackberries fatter than thumbs stained our fingernails.
Peaches squeezed out of their skins
and dripped into the lush weeds and crab grass.
Now winter squash lie on our pantry shelves,
nine left, like polished skulls hoarded in African huts
for good fortune. Tonight I am greedy for more

as I wait for the fire, reading seed catalogs
till I'm drunk on their promises. Hercules Butternut.
Silver Queen Corn. And a strawberry red as the sun
going down in my father's flat country
where he counts the last minutes, asking why
bother to take up his plow again, all it comes down
to is this, an old man with his stories
of good crops and bad crops,
one summer no rain and the next a flood
ripping out every last seedling.

Our fire catches, crackling like cornstalks
last August when wildfire swept over his dry acres.

Smoke hovered all day,
as if Georgia lay under siege again.
"Sherman's come back," joked my father,
but nobody laughed. Were we thinking
the same thing, that next time
not only the cornfields will burn
but the flesh on our bodies?
And after the big fire,
the long winter nights with no sunrise,
not even the seeds in the ground safe.
Not even the earthworms.

A firecracker startles me.
Sirens. You pop the champagne cork
and hold up a glass.
"To the harvest," you say,
"To zucchini and pumpkin and cabbage."
I stop you: "To earthworms."
You laugh. And we drink
to the earthworms asleep in our garden.

For Jim on Siler's Bald

Dizzy with you on the edge,
after what seemed like hours of climbing
toward sunlight, I stepped
back and studied a hawk floating
over the valley like a kite

somebody let go of. Why speak
of life changing its seasons
again? How the hardwoods
bore leaves into view or
the bears brushed off sleep
like a cobweb to follow the light
growing long on the leafmold
where earthworms fished,
busy as fingers? That happened

as always. But wind?
I remember the hawk riding
on it to nowhere I knew
when we lay down in thin air
to sleep with the rest of the creatures
the earth was about to awaken.

Potatoes

Henry arrives with his roto-tiller
eager to please. Come March
in the mountains we all want a garden.
We'd grow one in stone
if we had to. But of course
we don't have to. The earth is obliging
and Henry digs rocks from the ground
like a prospector. All afternoon
he plows. Under that jungle
of weeds is good earth. We're surprised.
"Oh ye farmers of little faith," he laughs
and picks up a brown clod. "Potatoes,"
he says. "I can taste them already.
They'd grow here like grass." The dirt clings
to his fingers. Above our heads
Rocky Face Ridge takes the sun like a lover
and beams. "Good thing
I got this job done today," he says,
rubbing his big palms together
like flint. "Hard rain's coming
tomorrow." Today it is Friday.
Today, I keep saying. Today
and today. We live here
by this patch of plowed earth
and we'll eat potatoes all winter.

Peaches

I swatted flies snoozing on peach pits
while Elmer's black arms sweated into the kettle
she stirred till her spoon disappeared and we fished
it out, dripping orange treacle. If jam settled

hard in the pot, she'd say, "Somebody's thinking shoes
wandered to Tennessee." "Not mine,"
I swore on my grandfather's spoonfuls of peach glue
he gobbled like ice cream. I whined

there'd be none left for me while I poked my cold cabbage.
"The Good Lord preserve us," my grandmother sweetly exclaimed,
sliding sticky plates into the dishwater. Grabbing
her steel wool, she scrubbed till she shamed

me right out to the orchard to brood
on the harvest we'd gather tomorrow, as if I'd learn
good table manners from watching fruit rot where I stood
eating peaches until I was sick. Oh, the setting sun burned

in my dreams like a ripe Georgia Belle doomed
to fester all winter on scullery shelves!
In the morning I heard Elmer's voice croon
her peach-picking song as she sharpened her knives

on the whetstone. The clanging of kettle tops
rang through the house, and all morning the odor of peaches
kept sneaking upstairs like a ghost that won't stop
asking something more from you. "Well, I hope that teaches

you prudence," my grandmother said,
standing over me, wiping my brow with her apron
to make me feel fragile. I stared past her head
at the dressing room mirror beginning to fill up with sun

and said, "No Ma'am,
I'm still hungry," knowing I lied.
There was too much to waste! Cream
and sugar and sun. Too much sun in my eyes.

I Inherit the Light of My Grandmother's House

1

Ashes

Only the bathtub was left
where I once saw her wash her toes solemnly
under a small, naked light bulb that sang
as she sang, like the telephone wires serenading
the desolate fields. Overflowing with ashes,
it looked like an urn claiming all that was left
of the plain dinner table her three daughters coveted
more than her cabinets full of bone china
and white linen tablecloths, more than the chiffarobe
nobody thought was worth having, its drawers hard

to open and empty of heirlooms except
for a clove-studded orange daintifying
her underwear, greasy coins
knotted in handerchiefs, needles
left rusting in stray bits of cotton.

I sift through those ashes
as if she has left something for me, a piece
of the chamberpot she kept close by
the immense sway-backed bed, or a safety pin
she might have found on her doorstep
to fasten a wandering slip strap inside the damp lace
of her powdery bosom. I kneel
in the rubble to dig for her false teeth
as if I would put them to rest in a glass
by my bedside, no longer a spoiled girl

who pampers her little white fingers
with warm oil and wears gloves to bed,
but a woman who sits in her claw-footed bathtub
at midnight and sees on her palms blisters
swell like the scuppernongs she dreams of bringing
back home through the curtain of dust
and the corn stubble everywhere. She holds them
up to the meager light. I see them shine.

2

THIEVES

Take all you want,
she'd say, slicing the biggest cabbage
or filling a sack with too many tomatoes.
Her husband was taken away on a stretcher
that creaked, dressed in new silk pajamas
and sealed in a coffin. The next day she moved
to town, jungle of ferns and her four-poster bed
in the back of a pick-up truck. Thieves came
to loot the abandoned house, little
by little took all her old clothes, even took
her pressed rose petals crumbling in cheap Zane Grey novels.
They left many cigarette butts to burn holes

in her carpet and frighten us when we came back
every month to the homeplace. Were they in her bedroom
that night the hail pounded her tin roof
and shattered her window panes? Any thief
rifling her coat pockets should have gone down on his knees,
as if he'd heard the sky of the last judgment falling,

what she herself must have believed
when the lightning awakened her, slumped
in her armchair, the TV still going.
The picture was ripping apart with each blast.
(I remember the rending of sheets every April,
her bed full of rags, and how she caressed dull wood
for days until she made it kindle with light

through her brocaded windows.) Next morning
we drove her out to the rubble that still smoked.
She walked to the edge of it,
stirring the ruins with her walking stick,
looking for something.
Nobody knew what.

"Nothing there," she said,
prodding the broken glass,
blackened stone under her feet.
"They took it all," she explained
to us, nodding her head
like a child. "I knew they would."

GLORY

Over the back of her chair she would
shake it loose, tilting her head
toward our fingers excited as tadpoles
swept into a waterfall, leaping
again and again through that
downpour that crackled and curled,

and the whole time
she never moved once, unless pigs
wiggled under the fence
and began to root up her best flowers
or chickens attacked her tomatoes.

Cherokee hair,
it was wild, wild as brambles.
How we yearned to braid
it in place, fussing
over her head as if she were the queen
of the tasselling corn! But our handiwork
never held long as a snap
of our fingers. The hairpins fell out
and that heavy black hair tumbled
into our arms. Only she knew the way
to secure it with a twist of her hands
as she stood up
and walked to the kitchen.

CLOUD

She had a sink
but the basin sat always beside it,
plain white, turning yellow
a bit at the edges, no ornament
as you see these days in phony log cabins
and country-style mansions.
My grandfather filled it each morning

and lowered his scratchy face
to it. His hands cupped the cold water
as if he wanted to drink it,
or now that his hands have been crossed
on his cold breast for ten years,
to bless it. Time consecrates
that scene right down to the last

whisker shaved and deposited
carefully into the water he later tossed
out the back door with an old farmer's
sober finesse. There it goes
again, just missing rooster
or bird dog, or, worse, herself
dumping the slops

in the pigsty, then turning
to look at her house, the sun filling
it up like a milkbucket. "Look out,"
he's calling, and she sees the lathery water
float, little cloud
over the earth into which it has gone
like the twinkling of my grandfather's eye.

DREAM

So patiently
she named the patterns
for me, Rose
of Sharon, Rose
in the Wilderness, Rose
in the Garden, but never
the last, Rose
of Fire, petals
crashing around us
like roofbeams. The Last
Rose of Summer,
I warbled while I brushed
her long, fading
hair. Pluck
the gray ones, she
told me. I could not
so she did, for
she had been
beautiful. You will be
someday, she said,
nodding ever so
slightly. But I was
the smart one who studied
too hard. I knew
better than wait
on an old woman's
prophecy. To be a woman
and not beautiful, how
sad, I sniffled
as I watched the cows
lumber into the sky.

Sadder still to lose
beauty, its black petals
falling all night
in the garden
where I am an ugly girl
to whom this
old game still
matters: she loves me,
she loves me not.

SUNRISE

I never wanted her table
her chiffarobe
her Bridal Quilt promised to me,
the first grand-daughter.

Why do their ashes still haunt me,
relentlessly blowing away?
What I keep is what I must remember.
A white cloth
and how she set down on it
durable silverware. Windows
that saw clear to Kingdom Come.
Shadows I made
in the sandy yard. Grit
in my eyes. What

we drove toward that dawn,
house of wind,
house of nothing but wind passing through,

and the sky,
an enormous tub holding the sun.

PRAYER

May she wake on a Saturday morning,
wind through a raised window lifting
the sheer curtain.
It will be late June,
the bird-dogs beginning to bark
and the hens scrabbling out by the pump house.
She hears Kathryn sing in the next room
and Dick climb the unsteady steps to the porch
where my grandfather pulls on his workboots.
Their rocking chairs creak.
They swap stories of good crops for hours,

so she need not hurry.
The coffee pot's ready.
The house needs no cleaning.
And listen! The cornfields are rustling
like water. The summer
is only beginning, the day that's before her
no dream. Can't she smell the magnolias,
hear mourning doves call from the river?
She opens her eyes
and sits up,
wide-awake among what she has lost.

Oh, the ceiling above her,
the floor at her feet!
May she live in that homeplace forever.

KITCHEN SINK

Today she would change nothing,
not even the wallpaper peeling
like dead bark. Nor, outside, the shadows
approaching the yard where ants
toil like women in their houses of sand.
Never mind that the sun will be setting.

When she was young she felt afraid
of hard wind and the rain that unsettled the creek.
But the earth never left her,
not once did the floods reach her feet.
The reward of a long life is faith

in what's left. Dishes stacked on a strong table.
Jars of dried beans. Scraps of cloth.
And the ten thousand things of her own thoughts,
incessant as creek water. She has been able

to lay up her treasures on earth,
as if heaven were here, worth believing.
In the water her hands reach
like roots grown accustomed to living,

the roots of the cat-briar that hold to the hillside
and can never be torn free of this earth completely.

KATHRYN STRIPLING BYER has published six books of poetry. *The Girl in the Midst of the Harvest* was her debut poetry collection, published by Texas Tech Press in 1986 as part of the Associated Writing Programs Award Series, selected by John Frederick Nims. Since then, her collections have all been published in the LSU Press Poetry Series. *Wildwood Flower*, her second collection, was named the Laughlin Selection from Academy of American Poets, followed by *Black Shawl*, chosen by Billy Collins for the Brockman-Campbell Award, given by the North Carolina Poetry Society. *Catching Light* received the 2002 Poetry Book Award from the Southern Independent Booksellers Alliance, and *Coming To Rest* earned the Hanes Award in Poetry from the Fellowship of Southern Writers in 2007. Her most recent volume, *Descent*, also in the LSU Press Poetry Series, won the 2013 SIBA Book Award for Poetry. Her poetry, essays and fiction have appeared in journals and newspapers ranging from The Atlantic to Appalachian Heritage. She served as North Carolina's first woman Poet Laureate from 2005 through 2009. She lives in Cullowhee, North Carolina, surrounded by the Blue Ridge Mountains.

Cover artist HENRIETTA LADSON is both an artist and educator residing in south Georgia. Currently, she teaches art at Deerfield Windsor School but has also taught at Darton College, the Albany Museum of Art, and conducted workshops. In addition to her interest in education, she is an active artist working in watercolor, oil, and mixed media. Henrietta exhibits regularly in many local shows. Her work can be viewed on her website: www.henriettaladson.com.

CPSIA information can be obtained at www.ICGtesting.com
Printed in the USA
LVOW12s1018060316

477977LV00007B/766/P